Keep this pocket-sized ⌐ __
you are travelling around Devon.

Whether you are in your car or on foot, you will
enjoy an evocative journey back in time. Compare
the Devon of old with what you can see today
—see how the streets have changed, how shops and
buildings have been altered or replaced, look at fine
details such as lamp-posts, shop fascias and trade
signs. See the many alterations to the Devon
landscape that have taken place during our lives,
and which we may have taken for granted.

At the turn of a page you will gain fascinating
insights into Devon's unique history.

FRANCIS FRITH'S
pocket ALBUM

DEVON

A POCKET ALBUM

Adapted from an original book by
DENNIS NEEDHAM

FRITH
BOOK CO

First published in the United Kingdom in 2003 by
Frith Book Company Ltd

ISBN 1-85937-711-4

British Library Cataloguing in Publication Data

Devon—A Pocket Album
Adapted from an original book by Dennis Needham

Frith Book Company Ltd
Frith's Barn, Teffont,
Salisbury, Wiltshire SP3 5QP
Tel: +44 (0) 1722 716 376
Email: info@francisfrith.co.uk
www.francisfrith.co.uk

Printed and bound in Great Britain by MPG, Bodmin

Front Cover: Sidmouth, The Esplanade 1918 / 68739
*The colour-tinting is for illustrative purposes only, and is not intended to be
historically accurate.*
Frontispiece: Lynmouth, Cherry Bridge 1907 / 59424

CONTENTS

FRANCIS FRITH
VICTORIAN PIONEER

Francis Frith, founder of the world-famous photographic archive, was a complex and multi-talented man. A devout Quaker and a highly successful Victorian businessman, he was philosophic by nature and pioneering in outlook. By 1855 he had already established a wholesale grocery business in Liverpool, and sold it for the astonishing sum of £200,000, which is the equivalent today of over £15,000,000. Now in his thirties, and captivated by the new science of photography, Frith set out on a series of pioneering journeys up the Nile and to the Near East.

INTRIGUE AND EXPLORATION

He was the first photographer to venture beyond the sixth cataract of the Nile. Africa was still the mysterious 'Dark Continent', and Stanley and Livingstone's historic meeting was a decade into the future. The conditions for picture taking confound belief. He laboured for hours in his wicker dark-room in the sweltering heat of the desert, while the volatile chemicals fizzed dangerously in their trays. Back in London he exhibited his photographs and was 'rapturously cheered' by members of the Royal Society. His reputation as a photographer was made overnight.

VENTURE OF A LIFE-TIME

By the 1870s the railways had threaded their way across the country, and Bank Holidays and half-day Saturdays had been made obligatory by Act of Parliament. All of a sudden the working man and his family were able to enjoy days out, take holidays, and see a little more of the world.

With typical business acumen, Francis Frith foresaw that these new tourists would enjoy having souvenirs to commemorate their days out. For the next thirty years he travelled the country by train and by pony and trap, producing fine photographs of seaside resorts and beauty spots that were keenly bought by millions of Victorians. These prints were painstakingly pasted into family albums and pored over during the dark nights of winter, rekindling precious memories of summer excursions. Frith's studio was soon supplying retail shops all over the country, and by 1890 F Frith & Co had become the greatest specialist photographic publishing company in the world, with over 2,000 sales outlets, and pioneered the picture postcard.

FRANCIS FRITH'S LEGACY

Francis Frith had died in 1898 at his villa in Cannes, his great project still growing. The archive he created continued in business for another seventy years. By 1970 it contained over a third of a million pictures showing 7,000 British towns and villages.

Frith's legacy to us today is of immense significance and value, for the magnificent archive of evocative photographs he created provides a unique record of change in the cities, towns and villages throughout Britain over a century and more. Frith and his fellow studio photographers revisited locations many times down the years to update their views, compiling for us an enthralling and colourful pageant of British life and character.

We are fortunate that Frith was dedicated to recording the minutiae of everyday life. For it is this sheer wealth of visual data, the painstaking chronicle of changes in dress, transport, street layouts, buildings, housing, engineering and landscape that captivates us so much today, offering us a powerful link with the past and with the lives of our ancestors.

Computers have now made it possible for Frith's many thousands of images to be accessed almost instantly. The archive offers every one of us an opportunity to examine the places where we and our families have lived and worked down the years. Its images, depicting our shared past, are now bringing pleasure and enlightenment to millions around the world a century and more after his death.

DEVON

AN INTRODUCTION

TUCKED AWAY in the west country of England, the county of Devon is often regarded as little more than a holiday destination, but the county has a rich historical heritage that can inspire and delight the visitor.

For years, Devon was the second largest county in England. Then, in 1974, boundaries were redrawn and the largest county, Yorkshire, was divided into three separate units. But that did not make Devon the largest county, for in the north, Cumberland and Westmorland were combined to form Cumbria, and so Devon remained runner-up. The population of just over a million is concentrated in the south of the county, where its two great cities, Exeter and Plymouth, are located. There is also the 'Riviera Coast' to the south, which centres on Torquay. The north of the county was a rural backwater until the 1980s, when a new road was built linking the M5 motorway with Barnstaple. This re-opened routes to such places as Ilfracombe and

Bideford, which had lost their rail services and had been quite remote until then.

Tourism brings considerable prosperity to the county. But Devon has a surprising diversity of commercial activity as well. Agriculture is another important part of the county's economy, with both sheep and dairy farming figuring prominently. In the wilderness of Dartmoor, and the larger part of Exmoor within the county boundary, arable potential is limited. But to the east, the red soil produces potatoes, and by the end of each summer there are fields of golden cereal crops awaiting the attention of the harvester. Mining also plays a role. Kaolin and ball clay are produced from rich beds in

BIDEFORD, FROM ACROSS THE RIVER TORRIDGE 1899 / 43077

both the south and west of the county. Much of this is exported, with Teignmouth the busiest port in Devon. Bideford is also still an active port, with ships going to the continent, and especially to Spain. Honiton lace and Dartington glass are two of the more specialised craft industries of Devon.

Cider is another craft activity; only one sizeable producer remains in Winkleigh. What is produced there is of the highest quality and should be approached with caution by the inexperienced. What might appear a delicious lunchtime pint can leave your legs developing a mind of their own, while an overpowering desire to sleep manifests itself. The cream tea—scones, jam and Devonshire cream—is another of the county's delights: never, however, call it 'clotted cream', for the manufacturing processes involved in making clotted cream in Cornwall and Devonshire cream are different. Cornwall scalds only the cream, and Devon the whole of the milk.

The scenery of this most gentle of counties is of an almost infinite variety. The lush green pastures of the Exe Valley around Cullompton are in striking contrast to the stark tors of Dartmoor. The river Tamar, dividing Cornwall and Devon for much of its length, has muddy flats at the lower end, wooded slopes higher up and craggy promontories on each side. The bridges that cross this river are sheer poetry to the eye. The Saltash railway bridge, designed by the great Isambard Kingdom Brunel, was an engineering wonder when it was built. The Saltash Road Bridge alongside carries more people today, but does not compete for beauty with Brunel's masterpiece. A little higher up the Tamar, another railway crossing at Calstock sweeps elegantly across the water. The train ride from Exeter to Newton Abbot is a memorable experience. Along the estuary of the Exe and beside the sea wall to Dawlish are major wintering habitats for migratory birds. Several short tunnels are linked by another wall, which is frequently damaged by winter storms roaring up the

English Channel. Many a train has had a severe salt washing while travelling along this section, which is one of the most spectacular in the country. For lovers of sheer beauty, Lydford Gorge is essential. A short walk up the gorge reveals a waterfall almost 100ft high, steep ravines, the Devil's Cauldron whirlpool and some ancient oak woods.

But Devon is nothing if not a seafaring county. It has produced many of our most famous sailors. Francis Drake was born near Tavistock, and Walter Raleigh near Sidmouth. That most famous of paintings, 'The Boyhood of Raleigh', was painted by Sir John Millais on the sea wall at Budleigh Salterton. All around its coasts small boats put out to sea, trying to wrest a living from the often unfriendly

EXETER, EXE BRIDGE 1929 / 82300

waters. Big ships are to be seen, too. Plymouth is a major ferry port with daily sailings to Roscoff in Brittany and regular crossings to Santander in northern Spain. The Navy are always active in Plymouth Sound, making the city a ship-spotter's paradise. Another of Devon's famous rivers is the Dart. Rising in Dartmoor Forest, it flows for 36 miles south towards the English Channel. At its southern end, the river is a magnet for yachtsmen. Pleasure boats also ply the river from Dartmouth and Kingswear up to Totnes. On this section of river, near Dittisham, the writer of detective thrillers, Agatha Christie, lived until her death in 1976.

The north of Devon is altogether more rugged. Cliffs and jagged rocks thrusting out into the sea make this a most inhospitable coastline. From the north-facing shore of Lynmouth as far as Ilfracombe, there is little refuge. Lynmouth now presents a calm face. But disastrous events on 15 August 1952 brought the village to the world's notice. It had been a particularly wet August, and Exmoor, high above the village, was waterlogged. Then a 22-hour period of heavy rain culminating in an enormous thunderstorm created nine more inches of rain by that Friday night. It ran straight off the land, flooding the East and West Lyn rivers. Some years before, where the twin rivers meet in Lynmouth, the West Lyn had been diverted and culverted into the East river, which it joined at right angles. But that night the culverts were blocked, and the East and West rivers came together in a boiling, angry torrent. A wall of water crashed through Lynmouth, spreading across the delta and wreaking destruction on everything in its path. By dawn on Saturday, the water level had dropped and the true extent of the devastation was revealed. Thirty-four people had died, dozens were homeless and a similar number of buildings were damaged or demolished. Today, there is little evidence of the ferocity and horror of that night, and the beautiful twin rivers run safely.

Ilfracombe is one of the departure points for the ferry to Lundy, a delightful island 18 miles out in the Bristol Channel. The other departure point for Lundy is Bideford on the river Torridge. The estuary here, where Torridge meets Taw, is a popular holiday spot. There are many lovely old villages. Appledore offers a nostalgic mixture of fishermen's cottages, pubs and narrow winding lanes. Along the coast to the west is the picturesque and justly famous village of Clovelly. Here wreckers used to ply their evil trade. Lanterns were tied to a donkey's tail and the beast was encouraged to walk along the cliff top. Mistaking this moving light for another ship, a captain would assume that this was a safe haven, with fatal results.

The Torbay coast draws the most visitors because of its scenic beauty and temperate climate. There are 22 miles of coastline from St Mary's Bay to Maidencombe. Torquay itself is a mass of hotels and guest houses. It acquired a certain cachet in the last century when the Napoleonic wars prevented people from travelling abroad. The extent and form of the town was established in those long-gone days. If Torquay is sophisticated, Paignton is a little more brash. Most of the town is given over to holidaymakers. One building of architectural interest is Oldway Mansion, built in 1873 by the Singer sewing machine owner. It is partially modelled on the Paris Opera House. The drama of the architecture was mirrored by the scandal caused when the American dancer Isadora Duncan came to live in the house with Singer's son.

Steam train enthusiasts will enjoy Paignton. Alongside the station is the start of a private railway to Kingswear. The old Great Western line was a popular route and offered one anomaly: the railway company built a station in Dartmouth, but there were no trains to serve it. Passengers came down to Kingswear and then crossed the river on a ferry.

There were plenty of fishing boats in what used to be known as Beer Roads. The rocky promontory, East Ebb, divided Seaton from Beer and kept the two places apart. The many caves in the cliffs offered smugglers discreet hideaways. One of Devon's most notorious smugglers, Jack Rattenbury, lived locally two centuries ago.

BEER

THE BEACH 1898 / 42434

The parish church of St Michael was built in 1878 on the site of an older chapel. Beer is famed for its quarries, which were worked by the Romans and have continued in use down the years. The stone was used extensively for the arcades of many Devon churches.

BEER

THE VILLAGE 1922 / 72946

SIDMOUTH

THE ESPLANADE 1918 / 68739

The red sandstone cliffs in the picture rise to 500ft on either side of the river Sid's valley. The town was one of many that became popular during the Napoleonic wars when the rich could not travel to Europe. They found Sidmouth before Torquay and it developed accordingly.

That the area is not disfigured by Victorian brickwork is an indication of how slowly the town developed. The varied façades create a flowing and pleasing harmony. Only the parish church suffered, being almost completely rebuilt in 1859 in a rather plain style.

SIDMOUTH

HIGH STREET 1906 / 53807

An indication of the lack of visitors to Sidmouth can be gleaned from this picture, taken from the Esplanade. The sea wall was constructed in 1835 and the shingle beach can be clearly seen. Overlooking the sea are some fine old cottages, exuberant in design and with bulging thatch.

SIDMOUTH

WEST END 1904 / 52069

17

*As a seaside town, Budleigh has developed almost
entirely since the beginning of the eighteenth century.
It was known as Saltre in 1210, and had become
Salterne by 1405. The names were derived from the
salt pans, which were located on the river Otter.*

BUDLEIGH SALTERTON

HIGH STREET 1898 / 42453

BUDLEIGH SALTERTON

HIGH STREET 1918 / 68726

Topsham, on the river Exe, is truly ancient. The Romans used it as their port to service Exeter, a function it continued to provide for centuries. By the date of this picture, its working days were over, leaving a pleasant riverside town, well loved for its ornate architecture.

TOPSHAM

THE QUAY 1906 / 53990

A typically busy picture of Dawlish beach. The rich variety of reds in the sandstone cliff are a delight to the eye. Brunel's seaside railway runs in and out of the cliffs through five narrow tunnels, offering a breathtaking ride for travellers to Paignton and Torquay.

DAWLISH

THE BEACH 1922 / 72990

An overview of Teignmouth, taken from Shaldon Hill, across the estuary of the river Teign. The town is said to be Devon's oldest resort. The commercial port was, and is, to the left of the picture. The navigation channel is so unstable that pilots check it after each tide.

TEIGNMOUTH

FROM TORQUAY ROAD 1890 / 26021

TEIGNMOUTH

FROM THE PIER 1903 / 49560

This photograph shows the holiday season in full swing. The bathing huts will soon be winched down to the shallows so that modest ladies can paddle discreetly. It is surprising to learn that the town was bombed repeatedly during the last war and an amazing 3% of the population were casualties.

This quiet little corner is on the north side of Torquay and reached by way of a romantic wooded ravine. There is no beach here, but the Victorians were determined to make the most of the warm waters. The bathing machine, sunk to its axles in the shallows, allowed decorum to be preserved.

TORQUAY

ANSTEY'S COVE 1896 / 38609

TORQUAY

THE BEACH 1924 / 76401

Torquay has long been a magnet for holidaymakers from all over the country. Its gentle climate in all seasons has proved irresistible. Styled as the English Riviera, its beaches are in fact somewhat smaller than might be imagined. This crowded scene looks south along Torbay towards Paignton. Changing tents have replaced the earlier bathing machines.

TORQUAY

FLEET STREET 1906 / 54027

The ladies are dressed fashionably, but in the event of a storm the road surface would turn quickly into a quagmire which would surely dirty their smart clothes. A motor vehicle can be seen driving into the distance, but the horse still reigns supreme. In the background newly-built villas speckle the wooded slopes.

The grace of Fleet Street in the previous picture is counterpointed by the timeless nature of this rural view, taken the same year on the outskirts of Torquay, possibly at Cockington. Tumbrils and carts have been stored under a thatched shed, its ground floor open to the elements. To the right is a sizeable dung pile.

TORQUAY

A FARMYARD SCENE 1906 / 54016

Presumably, these Avro 504J float-planes caused a considerable stir when they arrived. They were part of a batch of 200 built by Avro for the Royal Flying Corps in 1916 and still carry their military markings, although the name on the side indicates some form of civilian activity.

PAIGNTON

PRESTON SANDS 1918 / 68533

BRIXHAM

THE HARBOUR AND PRINCE OF ORANGE MONUMENT
1891 / 28241

*Before being overtaken by Plymouth a couple of decades earlier,
Brixham was the leading fishing port in Devon. At one time,
there were almost 300 trawlers employing 1600 seamen.
Hundreds more workers on shore built and repaired the ships
and manufactured sails and clothing, whilst the women knitted
underwear and packed the fish.*

BRIXHAM

THE FISHING FLEET 1896 / 38893

Because the town had been so heavily dependent on the single industry of fishing, the Depression of the 1930s arrived in Brixham early. It was very fortunate that its popularity as a holiday destination brought it a welcome alternative source of income.

BRIXHAM

FORE STREET 1922 / 73032

Both the Town Hall, the stone building on the right, and the Bolton Hotel on the left, are still here today. Bolton Cross is a local name given to the meeting of Bolton Street, New Road, Middle Street and Fore Street. Children gather around the public drinking fountain.

BRIXHAM

BOLTON CROSS 1922 / 73033

DARTMOUTH

'New' Quay was actually built in 1585. Before that, ships tied up at the churchyard wall of St Saviour's, the tower of which, built in 1631, can be seen in the centre. The Castle Hotel, with its imposing castellated frontage, dominates the waterfront. Dartmouth was once one of England's greatest ports, exporting wool and cloth.

DITTISHAM

ON THE DART 1889 / 21617

Salcombe was preserved from wholesale development because it was never reached by the railway. Kingsbridge, five miles to the north, was the closest the line ever penetrated. With only a small beach to boast of it never attracted hordes of holidaymakers. The 19th-century church (right) is Holy Trinity.

SALCOMBE

FROM PORTLEMOUTH 1928 / 81014

The main use of the harbour appears to be for recreation. A few fishing boats once worked in the area, but there are no signs of them in this photograph, just a small pleasure boat. The harbour has no picturesque buildings and retains its old working character.

BOVISAND

THE LANDING STEPS 1925 / 78509

BARNSTAPLE

HIGH STREET 1903 / 49620

Barnstaple is an old silted-up port and was once a centre for the woollen industrty. Since Victorian times it has been a regional shopping centre. Here, the photographer is facing south towards Boutport Street. There is a welter of shop signs—the Victorian and Edwardian shopkeepers were never slow to advertise their wares. Note the awnings suspended from simple poles.

The Square lies at the north end of the Long Bridge. The building to the right is the red façade of The Athenaeum, built in 1888, which houses the museum and a collection of fossils. The gazebo was provided as a shelter for the horse-drawn cab drivers, who are plying for business alongside. Behind the ornate Albert Clock is the prestigious Imperial Hotel.

BARNSTAPLE
THE SQUARE 1903 / 49616

This view shows the end of Boutport Street, where it enters The Square. The large building in the distance is The Athenaeum. On the left is the Golden Lion Hotel, with its attractive twin shallow bays and decorative wrought-iron balcony.

BARNSTAPLE

THE ATHENAEUM 1906 / 56044

BARNSTAPLE

BUTCHERS' ROW 1919 / 69323

44

The delightful open-fronted small shops are still largely unchanged today. On the left is the Pannier Market, built in 1885, a grand construction with a wooden vaulted roof of cathedral-like proportions. Market Days are Tuesday and Friday. Friday is also Cattle Market day, and the town heaves with people, augmented in summer by visitors.

HONITON

A LACEWORKER 1907 / 58075

Honiton is renowned for its lace, and the royal christening robe, still in use today, was made here for Queen Victoria in 1841. The building on the right, opposite the church, is now used as a lace museum. Many of the pleasing late Georgian buildings in this picture are still standing.

HONITON

HIGH STREET AND ST PAUL'S CHURCH 1904 / 52109

47

This is a quiet scene away from the bustle of the main road from London to the West Country. The Methodist chapel is on the left, whilst ahead is a railway bridge. The station is to the right, on the old London and South Western Railway line from Waterloo to Exeter.

HONITON

NEW STREET 1904 / 52110

The original Charter for this busy market was given around 1250 at the time the town became a borough. Drovers urge their animals through the throng, farmers haggle, and the townspeople watch out for bargains. Honiton's population exploded during Victorian times, owing to its importance as a rail junction.

NEWTON ABBOT
THE MARKET 1925 / 78550

Located just across the road from the train station, the park is named after the Courtenays, who were responsible for much of the building in town (they owned most of the land). A spacious and popular recreation area, it is surrounded by elegant villas, mostly Italianate in style.

NEWTON ABBOT

COURTENAY PARK 1906 / 56576

NEWTON ABBOT

FROM DECOY 1906 / 56571

Another open area of Newton Abbot is Decoy, to the south of town. With playing fields, a recreation area, a lake and woodlands, it is very popular with the local townspeople. There are fine views over the town and to the wooded slopes beyond.

Okehampton was established near a Saxon site just after the Norman conquest. The church in the picture is St James. This was built as a chantry chapel to All Saints, which was in the Saxon part of the town, well away from the newer area. Farmers gather at the corner to mull over the issues of the day.

OKEHAMPTON

FORE STREET MARKET 1890 / 22590

Tavistock is an ancient stannary town, renowned for its 10th-century Benedictine abbey. It was once the largest producer of tin in Europe. The delicate spire on the left was the Methodist church and is now demolished. The local constable poses stiffly in the left foreground. He may well have been a busy man—Tavistock had a reputation as a somewhat rough mining community, and the centre on Saturday nights could get a little lively.

TAVISTOCK

DUKE STREET 1890 / 22546

This gently curving street is to the east of the town. This view, looking back towards the town centre, shows both the Congregational and parish churches. The latter has three spectacular aisles, one built for the ancient Clothworkers' Guild with a roof of finely-carved beams and bosses.

TAVISTOCK

BROOK STREET 1910 / 62259

Tiverton is well blessed with open green spaces. With an old castle, and the River Exe running through the town, it presents plenty of opportunities for recreation. Here, family groups enjoy the sunshine and an old man sits alongside an ancient cannon.

TIVERTON

THE PARK 1903 / 49612

TIVERTON

ST PAUL'S STREET 1920 / 69889

This view looks towards the church from West Exe North. Set in an area of Victorian factory housing, these streets of modest but pleasing terraces are now part of a Conservation Area. Penny's, the corner shop, offers not only newspapers but fancy goods and a library.

57

TIVERTON

CASTLE STREET 1920 / 69888

Castle Hill is part of 365 acres of common land donated for '…the relief of the poor' in the 12th century. There are 20 miles of public rights of way. The river Torridge is to the left, and the straight line just to the right of it is the old course of the Rolle (or Great Torrington) canal.

TORRINGTON

CASTLE HILL 1890 / 24842

The gothic-style drinking fountain was presented to the town by the Honorable Mark Rolle in 1870. Beyond, the elegant arcade belongs to the Town Hall, jutting out into the street on stone piers, built in 1861. Torrington's prosperity was founded on wool.

TORRINGTON

MARKET PLACE 1893 / 32334

TOTNES

HIGH STREET 1896 / 38228

The ancient town of Totnes was once second only to Exeter as a prosperous merchants' town, but declined in importance in the 19th century. This view shows a lower view of the High Street. The covered walks, created by overhanging stories, were the location of two historic parts of the market area. On the right is the colonnaded and heavily shaded Poultry Walk; to the left is Butterwalk. Poultry was sold in the former, butter in the latter.

TOTNES

BUTTERWALK 1896 / 38227

The river Dart is one of the many delights of Totnes. Here a paddle steamer reverses off the landing stage. Trips down the river were as common then as they are today. It is regrettable that steam has given way to the internal combustion engine. Note the covered carriages waiting on shore.

TOTNES

THE 'TOTNES CASTLE' 1896 / 38216

EXETER

MOL'S COFFEE HOUSE 1906 / 53783

Exeter's spacious cathedral is 13th-century with earlier Norman towers. It suffered during the Dissolution and again at the hands of Cromwell's men. After two centuries of neglect, Sir Gilbert Scott restored it in the 1870s. The interior is magnificent with a breathtakingly beautiful ribbed vault.

EXETER

THE CATHEDRAL 1924 / 76579

These tall commercial buildings are still there today, marred somewhat by new frontages. Exeter was the furthest west that the Romans ventured. They halted on the banks of the Exe in about 50AD and founded the town of Isca. The West Country see was transferred to the safety of the Exeter city walls in 1049.

EXETER

HIGH STREET 1900 / 46043

*The High Street becomes Fore Street as it heads
down towards the river Exe. The street today is a
mass of shops and attractive buildings, none more
so than Tuckers Hall. This delightful building with
its stone-mullioned windows is a reminder of the
days when wool played an important role in the
local economy.*

EXETER

FORE STREET 1896 / 38008

The exquisite Guildhall is in the centre of this view of the High Street. It was built in 1330, remodelled in 1468, and the portico over the pavement added in 1592. The electric tram service, the tracks for which stretch along the road, was inaugurated in 1905.

EXETER

HIGH STREET AND GUILDHALL 1929 / 82291

EXETER

STEPCOTE HILL 1911 / 63678

EXETER

THE PORT 1896 / 38034

Graceful sailing ships are clustered alongside the quay on the Exeter Canal at the north end. The warehouse and Customs buildings around the Basin and riverside are beautifully preserved. In the background the city buildings rise over the rooftops.

Exeter's canal was built at the request of the Tudor merchants, who were exasperated by the weirs on the Exe that obstructed their vessels. It opened in 1566, and boasted the first pound locks in Britain. Originally just 16 feet wide, it was widened in the 1820s by James Green.

EXETER

FROM THE CANAL 1896 / 38033

PLYMOUTH

THE GUILDHALL AND POST OFFICE 1889 / 22388

The impressive Guildhall, a masterpiece of elaborate Victorian Gothic, was built in 1874. There had been three other such buildings previously. During the last war it was reduced to a mere shell but has since been restored to its original glory. Its tower is a noted land-mark over the city.

This picturesque area of narrow streets sits alongside the ancient fishing quay of Sutton's Pool. From here crowds watched the departure of the Pilgrim Fathers' vessel 'Mayflower' in 1620 on its voyage to the New World. The city's fish market was located here until the late 1990s, when it moved across the harbour to a new purpose-built dock.

PLYMOUTH

THE BARBICAN 1890 / 22474

In this busy scene Victorian ladies shelter from the sun under dark parasols. They must have been sweltering in their heavy gowns. Old Town Street, like so many Plymouth thoroughfares, was devastated in the war. Altogether, around twenty thousand Plymouth buildings were destroyed as a result of enemy bombing.

PLYMOUTH

OLD TOWN STREET 1889 / 22398

Bedford Street is another road that disappeared from the map following the blitz. It is clear that the Victorians remodelled much of the old city, constructing public and commercial buildings on a grand scale. Styled mostly in the preferred ornate Gothic, these additions sit awkwardly among the older, more urbane 18th-century buildings.

PLYMOUTH

BEDFORD STREET 1904 / 52407

The Lido and the walks were popular with the Victorians, and they offer beautiful views across the Sound. The lighthouse was rebuilt there, having been superseded by a more efficient building on the Eddystone rock south of the harbour. Close by is the world-famous Hoe.

PLYMOUTH

THE LIDO 1934 / 86216

Chagford is a tiny market town on the eastern slopes of Dartmoor, close to the upper reaches of the river Teign. With its jumble of streets and pleasing buildings of local moorstone, it has long been popular with visitors. Alongside the market place is the renowned Three Crowns Inn, where the poet Sidney Godolphin was shot during the Civil War.

CHAGFORD

MARKET PLACE 1906 / 56609

This cottage, probably 16th- or 17th-century, is typical of those found on the eastern side of Dartmoor. Its walls are hidden beneath some rather tatty rendering, but are almost certainly made of granite, which can be seen in the arch below the gable, and in the horse trough in which the little boy is standing.

LUSTLEIGH

WREYLAND, OLD COTTAGE 1906 / 56595

This tiny hamlet, tucked high up in the East Webburn river valley, huddles about its central green. St Pancras Church, with its lofty pinnacled tower, was built in granite in the 14th century. It was to come to Widecombe Fair that Uncle Tom Cobley borrowed Tom Pearce's grey mare.

WIDECOMBE IN THE MOOR

THE CHURCH AND VILLAGE 1907 / 5805

DARTMEET

THE BRIDGE AND A COTTAGE C1871 / 5530

Travelling here in 1871 would not have been a venture to take lightly: it was nearly fifteen miles' distance on unmade roads from Ashburton. The owner of this cottage may well have supplemented his income by providing a yoke of oxen to help pull carriages up the steep eastern bank of the Dart

The Rev W H Thornton, vicar of North Bovey in the latter half of the 19th century, was initially less than impressed with his flock: 'My new parishioners were very turbulent people ... the women were awful ... the whole village was much addicted to gossip of the worst description ...'

NORTH BOVEY

THE CROSS AT HELE FARM 1907 / 58515

In the distance is the hill of Brentor, topped by the 12th-century church of St Michael de Rupe, which was restored by the Duke of Bedford in the 19th century. In the foreground is the village of North Brentor; Christ Church was built in 1856 after it was decided that the long walk to the old church was too much for the poor delicate villagers.

BRENTOR

GENERAL VIEW 1908 / 59744

Knighton is now part of the sprawling village of Wembury which acts as a dormitory for Plymouth, but before 20th-century development it was part of a thriving farming community with many horses. The smithy, which closed in 1945, was run by the Colemans in 1907.

KNIGHTON

THE VILLAGE 1907 / 58501

Kingsteignton was for a long time the site of a mill which seemed jinxed. In 1795 it was attacked by a mob during bread riots, and in 1870 it had to be rebuilt after a fire. It is now a private house, and is reputed to be haunted.

KINGSTEIGNTON

THE VILLAGE 1906 / 56581

KINGSBRIDGE

THE PROMENADE 1920 / 69824

A paddle steamer loaded with trippers has just left for a voyage down the estuary. Steamers like this were a feature of many harbours in Victorian times, offering the first pleasure service to eager holidaymakers. Until the 19th century Kingsbridge was an important port for the shipping of wool and foundry products.

This old town is at the heart of a region of fertile farming country known as the South Hams. This view looks down the main street towards the tidal estuary extending up from Salcombe. The street is lined with a wide variety of buildings, including slate-hung houses with fine period shopfronts.

KINGSBRIDGE

FORE STREET AND BANK 1896 / 38507

ASHBURTON

TOWN CENTRE 1904 / 51202

The town lies just inside the Dartmoor National Park alongside the main Exeter to Plymouth road. Once stage coaches thundered through, forcing bystanders onto the narrow pavements. In grander and more prosperous days Ashburton was one of the region's strategic stannary towns. Mining finally came to a halt in the 19th century.

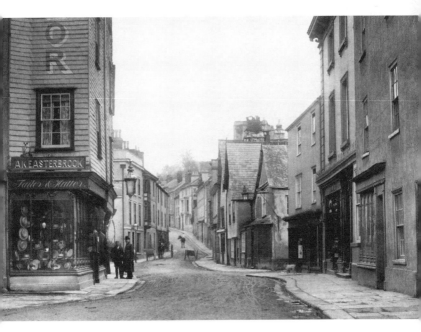

Alfington is a tiny village alongside the river Otter, north of Ottery St Mary. The narrow lane winds between thatched cottages, the fine example in the foreground featuring a tall chimney to carry the hot smoke safely away.

OTTERY ST MARY

ALFINGTON VILLAGE 1906 / 56678

Set in the midst of particularly fertile part of the county, Ottery had a market for centuries. John Coleridge was the Ottery vicar in the 18th century and his son, the poet Samuel Taylor Coleridge ('Rime of the Ancient Mariner' and 'Kubla Khan') went to school here. The awnings are down over the windows; it is a hot, sunny day.

OTTERY ST MARY

MARKET PLACE 1907 / 58182

The Girls' School (left) was originally called Oroolong, and was home to Captain Henry Wilson, discoverer of the Pelew Islands. The name comes from the island on which his ship, the 'Antelope', was wrecked in 1783.

COLYTON

FORE STREET, WITH THE GIRLS' SCHOOL 1907 / 58044

The London and South West Railway passed near here in 1860; but Talaton would have remained some distance from a station, had not the Sidmouth branch been built in the 1870s. Then Sidmouth junction was built, one of those odd stations that is several miles away from the place after which it is named.

TALATON

THE VILLAGE 1906 / 56675

There was a minster here as early as 705. Well before that, the Roman Fosse Way threaded its way through the town. In later years stage coaches halted at the 18th-century George Inn. The town is famed for its major carpet business, founded in 1755 by Thomas Whitty. Manufacture ceased in 1835 but began again in 1937.

AXMINSTER

TRINITY SQUARE 1902 / 48453

CLOVELLY

FROM THE HARBOUR 1906 / 55953

Clovelly hangs on the side of the hill, fringed by luxuriant woodland. Donkeys ply up and down the steep-stepped street, carrying goods on panniers.

CLOVELLY

MAIN STREET 1894 / 33490

The Pebble Ridge at Westward Ho! has much to commend it as a defence line against the Atlantic Ocean, which rolls relentlessly in its attempt to reclaim Northam Burrows which lie behind. Two miles long and 20ft high, it is a natural defence. Away from this, there are some pleasant stretches of sand.

WESTWARD HO!

PEBBLE RIDGE 1906 / 55961

APPLEDORE

THE RICHMOND DOCK 1923 / 75148

A view of the busy quay. Where the ships are tied up there is now an extended car park. This area was once noted for its shipbuilding, but only one yard survives today, with a sizeable dry dock. Out of sight round a bend in the River Torridge is Bideford.

APPLEDORE

THE QUAY 1923 / 75145

This charming Devon fishing village lies alongside the broad waters of the
Torridge River, which swings left just beyond the point to join the Taw and
the open sea. Though still in essence a fishing port, there are only a dozen
or so boats today, engaging in salmon-netting and deep-sea fishing. The pilot
boat for the estuary is also based here.

Bideford, two miles up-river from Appledore, is now the main commercial port in the area. Once the town manufactured and exported cloth and built ships; it imported tobacco and salted cod, and wool from the Continent for the Devon weaving industry. Today the quay is mostly used by the Lundy ferries.

BIDEFORD

THE QUAY 1890 / 24800

The view is still recognizable nearly a century later, although the houses on the left became a car park after a slum clearance programme in the early 1960s. East-the-Water is the settlement on the far side of the river. The railings must have provided welcome relief for the weary walker.

BIDEFORD

BRIDGE STREET 1906 / 55933

There was once a railway running down the middle of this street and around the corner at the end. It went to Westward Ho! and Appledore, and ran for sixteen years, closing in March 1917. The quay where ships tied up is on the extreme right.

BIDEFORD

THE QUAY 1919 / 69331

Old Ford Farm is virtually unchanged today. This is believed to be the oldest building in Bideford, dating from the 14th century. Less than half a mile upstream from Bideford Bridge, it is close by the original river crossing. This photograph encapsulates farming old-style, with hens running free in the yard by the house.

BIDEFORD

OLD FORD FARM 1890 / 24806

Instow is on the Torridge, opposite Appledore. Apart from a reinforced sea wall, this view of Marine Parade is little changed today. Here, visitors await the ferry for Appledore. The village is famous for its cricket club, which was established in the 1820s.

INSTOW

THE FORESHORE 1919 / 69337

WOOLACOMBE

GENERAL VIEW 1899 / 43130

The village is at the north end of a magnificent two-mile long sandy beach. Until the 1800s this stretch of coast was remote, its splendours familiar only to Ilfracombe fishermen. The roads inland were narrow and uninviting. It was only in the late Victorian era when builders began to throw up lines of villas overlooking the sea that Woolacombe's attractions were discovered.

Barricane Beach is behind the camera, and we see the broad expanse of Woolacombe sands stretching away south towards Croyde. The high ground to the right is Baggy Point, haunt of the peregrine falcon and once a fearsome threat to sailing ships. The hotels on the cliff above look out towards the island of Lundy almost twenty miles away.

WOOLACOMBE

FROM THE CLIFFS 1911 / 63938

The small beach to the left is at Prechers Rock. Before efficient transport links were opened to Ilfracombe, steamers crossed the Severn estuary from South Wales, discharging hundreds of day-trippers into the town. Today, the harbour is used by fishing boats, and in summer the 'Oldenburg' ferries visitors to Lundy.

ILFRACOMBE

CAPSTONE HILL AND THE PARADE 1911 / 63901

If the billowing empty deck chair is any guide, the wind is whistling up the Bristol Channel and through the Promenade Gardens. The crowds are already gathering around the bandstand for the afternoon matinee. To the left and behind is the Victoria Pavilion.

ILFRACOMBE

THE BANDSTAND 1923 / 74948

The outer pier, which provides access to Ilfracombe at any state of the tide, was not yet constructed. In this view, a pleasure steamer is berthed at the quay. The small building at the far end of the quay, below Lantern Hill, with the small chapel on top, is the lifeboat station.

ILFRACOMBE

THE HARBOUR c1890 / I50001

LYNTON

THE VALLEY OF THE ROCKS HOTEL 1907 / 59372

This 'convulsion of nature', close by Lynton, was highly popular with Victorian artists and writers, and other early seekers after the sublime and picturesque. Huge rocks lean precariously, the many stacks forming fantastic shapes that worked on the poetic fancy of early visitors like Wordsworth and Coleridge.

LYNTON

THE VALLEY OF THE ROCKS 1907 / 59384

*The pier was 18th-century, and the Rhenish tower added early in the
1800s by a General Rawdon. Here in the little town, hemmed in all
sides by majestic cliffs and headlands, the twin rivers of the Lyn join
together and race noisily out into the sea. Shelley praised Lynmouth's
unique scenic splendour in 1812.*

LYNMOUTH

THE PIER AND HARBOUR 1899 / 43095

LYNMOUTH

EAST AND WEST LYN RIVERS 1911 / 63855

Ships from South Wales carrying lime and coal were once regular visitors to the town. Paddle steamers from Bristol anchored out in the bay bringing trippers to enjoy the breezy heights of Lynton and Countisbury. Along the street in the picture was a special bath house, as well as a number of well-appointed new hotels and lodgings.

LYNMOUTH

THE HARBOUR c1930 / L126301

Tucked away among 'surroundings that are indescribably beautiful',
boats nestle in the placid harbour waters of this picturesque village
with its long, straggling street. Combe Martin's climate has been
praised: 'A stay here is wonderfully beneficial to those suffering from
threatened lung trouble'.

COMBE MARTIN
SCHOONER IN HARBOUR 1935 / 86745

COMBE MARTIN

VIEW OF THE VILLAGE 1930 / 83463

INDEX

PLEASE HELP US BRING FRITH'S PHOTOGRAPHS TO LIFE

Our authors do their best to recount the history of the places they write about. They give insights into how particular towns and villages developed, they describe the architecture of streets and buildings, and they discuss the lives of famous people who lived there. But however knowledgeable our authors are, the story they tell is necessarily incomplete.

Frith's photographs are so much more than plain historical documents. They are living proofs of the flow of human life down the generations. They show real people at real moments in history; and each of those people is the son or daughter of someone, the brother or sister, aunt or uncle, grandfather or grandmother of someone else. All of them lived, worked and played in the streets depicted in Frith's photographs.

We would be grateful if you would tell us about the many places shown in our photographs—the streets with their buildings, shops, businesses and industries. Describe your own memories of life in those streets: what it was like growing up there, who ran the local shop and what shopping was like years ago; if your workplace is shown tell us about your working day and what the building is used for now. With your help more and more Frith photographs can be brought to life, and vital memories preserved for posterity.

We will gradually add your comments and stories to the archive for the benefit of historians of the future. Wherever possible, we will try to include some of your comments in future editions of our books. Moreover, if you spot errors in dates, titles or other facts, please let us know, because our archive records are not always completely accurate—they rely on 150 years of human endeavour and hand-compiled records.

So please write, fax or email us with your stories and memories. Thank you!

CHOOSE ANY PHOTOGRAPH FROM THIS BOOK

for your FREE Mounted Print. Order further prints at half price

Fill in and cut out the voucher on the next page and return it with your remittance for £2.50 for postage, packing and handling to UK addresses (US $5.00 for USA and Canada). For all other overseas addresses include £5.00 post and handling.
Choose any photograph included in this book. Make sure you quote its unique reference number eg. 42365 (it is mentioned after the photograph date. 1890 / 42365). Your SEPIA print will be approx 12" x 8" and mounted in a cream mount with a burgundy rule line (overall size 14" x 11").

Mounted Print
Overall size 14 x 11 inches

Order additional Mounted Prints at HALF PRICE - If you would like to order more Frith prints from this book, possibly as gifts for friends and family, you can buy them at half price (with no extra postage and handling costs) - only £7.49 each (UK orders), US $14.99 each (USA and Canada).

* IMPORTANT!

These special prices are only available if you order at the same time as you order your free mounted print. You must use the ORIGINAL VOUCHER on the facing page (no copies permitted). We can only despatch to one address.

Have your Mounted Prints framed (UK orders only) - For an extra £14.95 per print you can have your mounted print(s) framed in an elegant polished wood and gilt moulding, overall size 16" x 13" (no additional postage).

FRITH PRODUCTS AND SERVICES

All Frith photographs are available for you to buy as framed or mounted prints. From time to time, other illustrated items such as Address Books, Calendars, Table Mats are also available. Already, almost 50,000 Frith archive photographs can be viewed and purchased on the internet through the Frith website.

For more detailed information on Frith companies and products, visit

www.francisfrith.co.uk

For further information, trade, or author enquiries, contact:

The Francis Frith Collection, Frith's Barn, Teffont, Salisbury SP3 5QP
Tel: +44 (0) 1722 716 376 Fax: +44 (0) 1722 716 881 Email: sales@francisfrith.co.uk

Voucher

for FREE
and Reduced Price
Frith Prints

Do not photocopy this voucher. Only the original is valid, so please fill it in, cut it out and return it to us with your order.

	Picture ref no	Page number	Qty	Mounted @ £7.49 UK @$14.99 US	Framed + £14.95 (UK only)	US orders Total $	UK orders Total £
1			1	**Free of charge***	£	$	£
2				7.49 ($14.99)	£	$	£
3				7.49 ($14.99)	£	$	£
4				7.49 ($14.99)	£	$	£
5				7.49 ($14.99)	£	$	£
				7.49 ($14.99)	£	$	£
Please allow 28 days for delivery				* Post & handling		**$5.00**	**£2.50**
				Total Order Cost		**US $**	**£**

Title of this book . . . .

I enclose a cheque / postal order (UK) for £ . . . . $ . . . .
payable to 'Francis Frith Collection' (USA orders 'Frith USA Inc')

OR debit my Mastercard / Visa / Switch (UK) / Amex card / Discover (USA)
(credit cards only on non UK and US orders), card details below

Card Number

Issue No (Switch only)   Valid from (Amex/Switch)

Expires   Signature

Name Mr/Mrs/Ms . . . .

Address . . . .

. . . .

. . . .

Postcode/Zip. . . . . Country . . . .

Daytime Tel No . . . .   Valid to 31/12/06

PAYMENT CURRENCY: We only accept payment in £ Sterling or US $.
If you are ordering **from any other country, please pay by credit card**, and you will be charged in one of these currencies.